A MIND OF CHEER

How the Philosophy of Cheerleading Can Be Applied Through All Aspects of Life

JORDAN L. BROWN

Dedicated to my friends, coaches, and family, including my cheer family.

A Mind of Cheer

Jordan L. Brown

Graphic Designs by Rachel Elizabeth Design

©2019 MindCheer LLC

In Association with:
Elite Online Publishing
63 East 11400 South Suite #230
Sandy, UT 84070
EliteOnlinePublishing.com

ISBN# 978-1695869202

Disclaimer: Readers, please do and try techniques at own risk. This book reflects the author's present recollections of experiences and thoughts over time.

This book does not push any type of religion or belief onto readers as it is from the author's personal experience.

The Win-Win Concept is inspired and stemmed from "The Win-Win Negotiation" created by, Former Harvard Law School Professor, Roger Fisher, and academic, anthropologist, and negotiation expert, William Ury, in their book, "Getting to Yes."

Contents

Yes to Cheer 7

Power of Positivity 13

We Got Spirit 21

Rebound Out of Fear & Failure 41

Inspirational Leaders 45

Pink Out 53

Adrenaline & Courage 57

Spirit Stick 59

Stunt Groups 65

Bows to Toes 73

C 79

Coaches & Mentors 85

It's Game Day 89

L-E-T-S G-O! 95

Halftime Performance 97

Megaphones 107

Elevate 109

Yes to Cheer

The purpose of this book is for each and every cheerleader to know the spirit they have within their heart is a true treasure within this world. The spirit, positivity, inspiration, and genuine heart of a cheerleader has extraordinary power to impact the world on a very high and elevating level. The heart, mind, and soul of an individual that is developed in cheerleading can release so much power within one's self in so many different ways. This book is to extend the qualities of being a cheerleader outside of cheer and into all aspects of life. There is a major happiness revolution on the rise in our world and I truly believe the magic is inside every single cheerleader's heart. Your mental ability is abundant. Your boundless energy is a phenomenon. The amount of creativity learned through cheers, stunts, and dances teaches us the vitality of teamwork and imagination. Cheerleaders develop very strong self-discipline, as well as flexibility that allows us to flow through living an amazing life.

My goal is for cheerleaders to never lose the qualities they develop through cheerleading. As I have been going through the adventures of life after cheerleading, I have kept the S-P-I-R-I-T alive in so many different ways. Cheerleaders are always motivating others, and for you who is reading this, I am here to cheer for you, guide you, and teach you how to transition everything you learn from our magical world of cheerleading to your life going forward. I remember as if it was yesterday, the first time I knew I wanted to be a cheerleader. Royal blue, vibrant red, and pure white pom poms stacked on backpacks displayed with the school mascot. There was a group of people with matching outfits, smiles on their face, glowing with positivity. I remember my mother picking my brother up from his football practice, and seeing such an uplifting group of people looking so happy and focused! I decided to try out for my high school cheer squad my freshman year. I was placed in a community, the school community, and I knew I wanted to be a positive light for the community. The positive leadership, standing up for the school and everyone who was part of it, bringing unity through positive actions were the core reasons of why I decided to try out for the cheer team.

Flash forward through high school and college, the night I secretly dreaded came upon me. It was the senior night of my beloved university. With three years experience as captain of my squad, my heart was filled with my team, coaches, school, and community. I deeply valued the connection with the community by being a happy and motivating role model. From weekly practices to early morning workouts, game days and pep rallys, community service to cheer camps, my whole life of cheer was all about to be gone. I was torn between feeling so much appreciation and love for cheerleading, to a bit fearful of what was to come next. Little did I know at the time, that the spirit, mind, and heart developed through cheerleading can prosper into true positive impact within our world.

Do you remember when you first decided you wanted to be a cheerleader? What was it? Who was it? How old were you? What made you decide, "Hey, I want to be a cheerleader!"? On the next page, I would like for you to write out what made you decide to pursue cheerleading. What was the experience? How did you feel? What inspired you to become a cheerleader? Journal your experience!

Journal Entry

A Contract of Cheer:

This is your personal contract of having a life full of cheer.
This allows you to commit to the positive spirit within.

I,_____, promise to live everyday with a
cheerful heart, strong work ethic, and exceptional spirit.

I,_____, promise to be thankful for every
single person who comes in my life, for they have a light within that
guides and connects to the light within myself.

I,_____, promise to cheer for others, as well as
myself, to reach their highest potential in all aspects of life.

I,_____, promise to cheer for the community to take
action in improving our world in the most positive way possible.

I,_____, promise to dream boldly, trusting my
mind, body, and soul to connect with the universe above, making my
dreams come true.

I,_____, promise to spread the positive spirit within
my heart to others to truly make a positive impact within the world.

_____   _____
Signature   Date

Power of Positivity

The power of positivity is a very important concept to embrace to truly grow a positive and prosperous life. There have been infinite amounts of research and studies on the value of having a positive attitude and mindset. By having positive thoughts, we can transform the world around us in a positive way. Like attracts like. Positivity attracts positivity! Being positive gives us an uplifting confidence that can truly move us through any situation.

There are very simple ways of shining positivity. For example, a negative mindset might say, "Oh my, it's raining outside and my hair is going to get messed up!" A positive mindset might say, "Oh my, it's raining outside and the plants and flowers around us are going to flourish into beauty..and I'm going to grab an umbrella." Positivity requires us to actively look at the bright side of a situation and allows us to create solutions so we can live on the bright side of life. The power of positivity invites us to say, "I CAN DO THIS. I WILL LIVE MY DREAMS. DREAM AND ACHIEVE." The emotions, thoughts, perceptions, reactions should focus on the positive, and move forward. This keeps the positivity flowing through us and outwards to our world.

Cheerleaders are always chanting positive cheers, cheering for their school, working hard to master techniques and skills. This all demonstrates how much of an impact can be made by focusing on the importance of being POSITIVE! One way cheerleaders practice positivity is by chanting cheers and chants. The concept of repeating a positive chant three to four times creates a positive energy flowing through the body and the environment around us. The positive energy connects within and we truly believe in the positive chants.

Cheers and chants are similar to positive affirmations. Affirmations are just like chants: they are statements that are repeated often to empower and overcome a certain situation or mindset. An example of a positive affirmation is, "I am brave and courageous!" Repeating this affirmation three to four times creates a positive mindset of being brave and courageous!

We must actively seek out positivity within situations. As a cheerleader, we routinely repeat sideline cheers at least three to four times! With this concept, we can turn the sideline cheers into positive affirmations. When we cheer, we FEEL it in our hearts, truly wishing the best for our school. When we apply the same concept and FEEL the positive affirmations, we are sending out the same spirit and energy. When I graduated college, I gradually turned towards positive affirmations without even realizing how incredibly similar they are to CHEERS! It was amazing to see the magical moments prosper into my life. Below, I would like for you to seek out positive affirmations that truly speak to your heart and write them down! Routinely, I would like for you to look at your affirmations, repeat them at least three to four times daily. Keep repeating and truly believe in them!

Positive Affirmations

"I lead with a passionate heart and demonstrate positive actions to bring happiness to others." *-JLB*

The WIN WIN Concept
Let's WIN! Think WIN WIN!

The Win Win Concept is a way to think positive and creates a space for everyone to win. In addition, the Win Win Concept can be applied in another light by taking any type of rejection as direction and turning any negativity into positivity, making it a win. If something does not work out, we often close ourselves off to any unknown opportunities that can be a result of that rejection. This causes us to miss the door opening after a door closes. It is important to welcome this magical space and trust the universe is guiding us more towards our destiny. In addition, rejection allows us to grow, learn, and redirect, which is all a major win! In another light, the Win Win Concept teaches us to root for others and to help others win as well. It is important to root for others to win. When one of us wins and we support someone else in their success, we again bring positivity into the world, which makes it a win for all! The Win Win Concept helps eliminate any type of jealousy or envy. It is important to gain perspective of what positive impact or influence one is making within the world and to acknowledge how we are all part of a shared humanity with unique gifts. Everyone has a unique spirit within their hearts. Therefore, we must root for them to have the light shine through to our world and to the stars above!

Positive & Growth Mindset
Below are different techniques to have a positive & growth mindset!

Negative	Positive
I'm not good at this.	This is an opportunity to learn.
I give up.	I'll use a different strategy.
I made a mistake.	I forgive myself and will learn.
Plan A didn't work.	I will try Plan B, C, D, E...
My friend can do it.	I will learn from my friend.
This is hard.	I will practice and become familiar.
I have no time.	I will use my time efficiently.
If you succeed, I'm threatened.	If you succeed, I am inspired.

Fixed	Growth
Avoids challenges.	Embraces challenges.
Ignores criticism	Learns from feedback.
Avoids work.	Worth the effort.
Gives up easily.	Never, ever gives up.
I am a failure.	Persistent through setbacks.
Rejection.	Direction.
Avoids failure.	Desires continuous learning.
Desires to look smart.	Confronts uncertainties.
EGO	EVO/ECO*

*EVO stands for evolve. ECO stands for ecosystem.

"I will make the world a better place with my compassionate heart, resilient work ethic, and positive spirit." *-JLB*

We Got Spirit

Our love, drive and positivity all combine together to create an energy, a force within ourselves that can only be described as passion. It connects us with the world around us, with our universe, even and yells out, "YES, WE GOT SPIRIT!" We channel that passion into a wave of high energy over the crowd and truly uplift our society. It is important to extend that type of passion and energy from cheerleading into all areas of life. We can channel that energy towards goals, aspirations, and visions! Passion mixed with purpose is a true game changer. Passion creates a strong energy, a drive, within oneself to truly accomplish and connect with their purpose. Combining your purpose and passion together creates true magic within one's self and connects with the world.

On the next page, there is a specific diagram in the form of a cheerleading bow, based off of the Japanese concept called Ikigia, which means "reason to live." When a very influential friend shared this concept with me, I thought, "How amazing. I must share this message with others." The diagram has been modified into a cheerleading bow to represent all of our individual interests, goals, aspirations outside ourselves, and internal thoughts. Once the ribbon is tied, pulling everything together, it creates the knot, the center of the bow, which represents your purpose. In some ways, it's like a gift. A cheerleading bow is like a bow on top of a present. It is your gift. The four segments of the bow, and the purpose in it's center, teaches us to be fully present within our lives and our purpose.

Now it's your turn. In each section of the bow, write down qualities you believe are most important to you. Once finished, choose the top 2 qualities from each of the four sections to connect with each other and design your purpose. From that work, you should be able to come up with a purpose statement for your life. What do you want to accomplish and achieve within your life? Once you have determined your purpose statement, write it down and make it your commitment to yourself to take that on as your purpose!

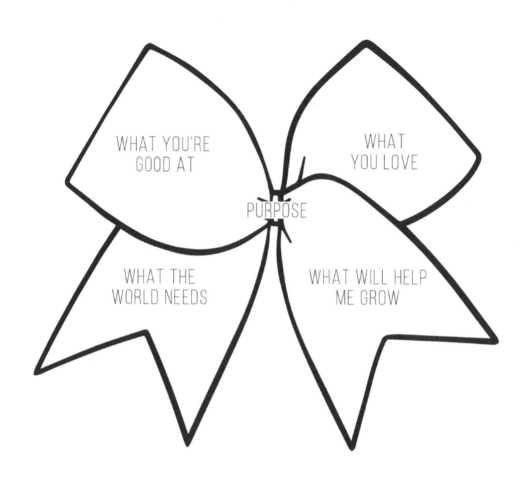

YOUR PURPOSE   THE GIFT   BE PRESENT

Write your top 2 for what you are good at:

    1.

    2.

Write your top 2 for what you love:

    1.

    2.

Write your top 2 for what will help you grow:

    1.

    2.

Write your top 2 for what the world needs:

    1.

    2.

Purpose Statement

Combine your gifts from above to make your own personal purpose statement! This can be as detailed as you wish. When creating your purpose statement, channel your inner passions and release the magical power within to our amazing world! Let's write your purpose statement!

_____

_____

_____

On the next couple of pages, there is a mind map and a vision board created for you to fulfill with your thoughts, dreams, and passions. There are several ways to fill out a mind map. One easy way is to connect qualities and habits to different senses. The purpose of a mind map is to create a mindset you wish to attain in all aspects of your life. For example, for using your sense of sight as a reference, seeing, the eye, think of habits, qualities, and techniques that involve the eye. For example, you may write to see the beauty in every day life, look for where others need help, make eye contact when speaking with others, visit the eye doctor for a check-up. For each category, you will write down different ways you wish to improve that category. For the vision board, you will draw out or cut out pictures you will have in your life, either in the near future or down the road. This creates a visual for your mind to connect thoughts to action, creating an opportunity for you to reach your goals!

MIND MAP

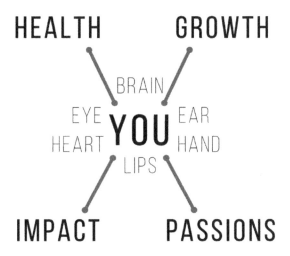

VISION BOARD

LIFE OVERVIEW MODULE

0
_____

_____

_____

_____

30
_____

_____

_____

60
_____

_____

_____

90

Above is a life overview module. This demonstrates the years of your life from beginning to end. For each of these periods, I would like you to set different goals for yourself, and note any achievements you have already accomplished so far in your life. While your goals may change over time, this helps remind you of the importance of time and living a fulfilling life.

THE LAW OF ATTRACTION

- VISUALIZE THE DREAM LIFE
- POSITIVE AFFIRMATIONS
- REPETITION AND INTENTION IS KEY
- VISUALIZE SUCCEEDING IN YOUR GOAL
- YOU ARE WHO YOU THINK
- ALIGN ACTIONS WITH GOALS
- PRACTICE GRATITUDE DAILY
- BELIEVE IT WILL HAPPEN
- BE PATIENT
- ALWAYS GIVE MORE TO OTHERS
- FOCUS

POM POM MAGIC

On the next page are categories of pom poms. For each pom category, list different interests, qualities, and ideas that really bring out your happiness. Once you have a few written down, think about combining different sets of poms, showing how the qualities of one pom can coordinator with and positively accentuate the qualities of the other pom. For example, for the social pom, you may put friends or networking, and then for impact, you may put positive impact or helping the local community. The way you would match the poms of impact and social could be to set up a night in with your friends, having everyone bring clothes they would like to donate to a local women's or men's center. Creating an innovative mindset allows us to link multiple passions together and develop a more exciting purpose.

HEART

SOCIAL

IMPACT

MIND

HEALTH

ADVENTURE

MIX & MATCH YOUR POMS

_____

_____

_____

_____

_____

_____

_____

_____

_____

_____

_____

"The true sign of intelligence is not knowledge but imagination."
- Albert Einstein

Mind, Body, & Spirit

When we participate in cheerleading we have to use our mind, body, and spirit. Transitioning this into other aspects of our lives allows us to truly enrich every aspect of our lives. In my own transition from cheerleading to other adventures, I have learned how to channel my energy and develop a positive mind, along with physical activity, through yoga. Yoga is similar in a way to cheerleading. We are focusing on physical positions, uplifting others within the room, improving our mindset, and connecting positive energy to the world. Within cheerleading, we focus on projecting our voice and use our breath. Breath is so important in cheerleading because it allows us to chant to the crowd while doing so many different moves, stunts, and tumbling. Similarly, in yoga there is also a focus on our breath. Hitting multiple positions while focusing on breath. Giving infinite appreciation for breath is EVERYTHING. Being so thankful for the simple act of breathing alters our perspective and gives us infinite amounts of gratitude.

After I graduated college, I moved from Illinois to Maryland, and during my time in Maryland, it was very hard for me to meet people. However, during that time, I really focused on my spirituality, body, and skill sets. A year after living in Maryland, I moved to California. I was referred by a friend to join a gym, which had a lot of incredible yoga classes. I was interested in trying all of them, so I would go to different classes during the week. One of my amazing instructors is named Rachel, who is also a former university cheerleader. With cheerleading being such a big part of my life, I felt a strong sense of comfort and belonging around her. Since I felt this way, I was motivated to attend classes regularly, which helped me create not only a very strong dedication to my yoga practice, but also helped me build a sense of community. Rachel has always been a huge inspiration as she is an international yoga instructor teaching classes and retreats around the world! Excitedly, Rachel has shared her story with us about her life with cheerleading and yoga!

Rachel's Journey

I found yoga after my nine year cheerleading career ended. I cheered from 8th grade all the way until my senior year at Missouri State University. Cheerleading was my identity, but when college was over, all of a sudden that book had closed and I was left wondering what I was going to do with all of this free time.

I had two friends, Nikki and Stephanie, who were former cheermates at MSU, who were teaching at a new yoga studio in town, and they invited me to come take a class. Now, yoga wasn't really a popular thing where I'm from, so doing yoga was never really a thought for me. Springfield, Missouri is a pretty standard, conservative Midwest town, and I'm pretty sure this studio was one of the first!

I started going and almost immediately fell in love with the practice. What initially drew me to yoga were the physical aspects, but it also became clear to me that there were far more benefits to the practice of yoga than just fitness. Yoga grounds and centers you, and helps you find that important connection between mind, body, and breath where you can get into a flow state. A state of flow in yoga can be similar to going through a routine in cheerleading, where you are so present in the moment and your mind is focused that it can't wander to anything else. The mental, emotional, and spiritual sides of yoga are, to me, the most beneficial aspects of the practice.

Not long after I moved to California, I really started going deeper into my yoga journey. I became a certified yoga instructor myself and now teach regularly every week, and lead workshops and international yoga and adventure retreats. I also found a practice called acro yoga, which is a blend of acrobatics and yoga, done with a partner. Being a former cheerleader, this of course is right up my alley! Having body awareness and control is definitely a benefit to this practice. It's fun, challenging, and really requires trust and communication with your partner, much like cheerleading.

I have now been practicing yoga for 12 years, and I can most certainly say I only wish I found it while I was cheering. It would have been such a benefit to not only have had the increased flexibility, but also the mental clarity, the control of breath, and the many other important tools that yoga provides. I have found something that I love as much as I loved cheerleading. Yoga is my passion and my purpose and has not only expanded my physical abilities, but it has expanded every other area of my life!

Meditation

Another tool that involves our breath that can have a major impact on our lives is meditation. With meditation we can grow and enrich our spirit. Why meditation? It allows us to think clearly without distractions pulling our attention. We connect back with ourself, and have a more clear connection with our intuition and self. The meditation concept can be explained by imagining a pom pom. The pom pom has a million different strands. In the center of the pom pom is a handle. We can think of our thoughts as the strands of the pom pom and our mind as the handle. The handle does not move as the strands of the poms do. We must separate the attention-getting thoughts from our minds. Meditation allows us to focus on simply being, like the stable pom handle at the core. Meditation allows us separate those attention-getting thoughts from our mind, and creates a still, calm and solid state of being.

ATTENTION - GETTERS

MIND

"The more you praise and celebrate your life, the more there is in life to celebrate!"

-Oprah Winfrey

GRATITUDE JOURNAL

Write 3 things you are grateful for today...

What's a simple treasure you are grateful for...

What opportunities are ahead of you that you are grateful for...

Open the door, look outside. Write 3 things you see that you are grateful for...

What is something you have today that you did not have a year ago...

Write a cheerful memory..

Rebound Out of Fear & Failure

There was a time when I was learning how to do a round-off backtuck. I remember very distinctively my coach telling me to think of the body as a broom bouncing off the floor, meaning to straighten the body once landing a round-off. The whole concept of a broom bouncing off the floor being the rebound is similar to the connection of a ball hitting the ground. The harder the ball hits the ground, the higher it bounces up into the air.

In some ways, fear and failure are very similar to that bouncing ball or broom. When they arrive in our life, we feel very low and see everything as being very hard. For you reading this, please know fear and failure are natural parts of human life. With fear, I would like for you to acknowledge the feeling as temporary, accept yourself for feeling the emotion, take a deep breath, separate your mind from the emotions, and then let courage fill every cell within the body and know that you are not alone. You got this!

When it comes to failure, everyone has experienced some level of setback. But rather than seeing it as a negative, try to welcome failure as a launching pad for what is to come next. Like the broom and ball, the harder it hits the ground, the higher it bounces up into the sky.

When setbacks present themselves, there may be a period of time afterwards that seems very low, confusing, and sad. However, this is a time where a lot of energy is building up for you to prosper. Practicing self-care tips, meditation, giving back to the world, applying your heart, and giving yourself a pep talk are important during this time to help you work through the difficulties and to bounce back. Taking it step by step, and allowing yourself to heal gives you the strength to come back stronger than ever.

THE PEP TALK

-TAKE A DEEP BREATH IN

-ACKNOWLEDGE FEELINGS

-ACCEPT FEELINGS

-SEPARATE YOUR MIND

-KNOW YOU ARE CAPABLE

-TRUST YOURSELF

-SAY, "I GOT THIS!"

-TALK WITH A TRUSTING FRIEND

-IMAGINE YOUR FUTURE SELF CHEERING FOR YOU

-GIVE YOUR FUTURE SELF A WINK!

Inspirational Leaders

L eadership is an important component of cheerleading. Cheerleaders are just that: cheer leaders! The leadership component of being a cheerleader isn't just about standing up and leading the school in cheers. It's also about standing up for others and being an ideal leader to every person within the school! For example, if there is someone being bullied, stand up for them! I remember in high school, there was a new student who sat alone on their first day. Automatically, I stood up and sat by her, and simply asked her where she was from and got to know her. As it happened, we became very close friends throughout our high school years.

This simple action of going over to welcome a new student built courage within my heart to go up to people, who I do not know, and make conversation in social settings. In addition, it taught me to be assertive with my values. There is a difference between being assertive and being a-g-g-r-e-s-s-i-v-e. Being assertive means to speak honestly and compassionately about your personal morals, values, beliefs, and thoughts. As a cheerleader, it is part of one's responsibility to be positive, assertive, and outgoing leaders for the school.

There are infinite ways of being a positive leader. Within a squad, there are multiple personalities present, which allows us to experience a variety of personalities and talents from each other, as everyone has their own special gift. A positive leader helps share their perspective of how to help make positive impact within the team and community.

It is important to understand everyone has their own perspective and view. We must accept each other, motivate each other, and believe in one another, all while understanding, respecting and valuing each others' differences. This allows us to gain perspective and insight. We cheer for our teammates and everyone's individual gift. We cheer for our friends and their dreams. Not only do we support our teammates, but also we cheer for our team, our school, our community.

We are MOTIVATORS. We motivate others to accomplish their goals, to win, to be the best they can be. It is part of us to cheer for each other and our community. Not only do we inspire others, but we motivate with strong leadership! When we have confidence in others, we motivate them to truly believe in themselves to make their dreams come true. Throughout history, we have had incredible inspirational leaders. From Walt Disney to Martin Luther King Jr, we have learned to believe in our visions and strive for the most positive impact for our world. Being an inspirational leader goes above and beyond for our society. It is important to value this gift within and to strive in making a difference in the lives of others.

"I work hard to make a cheerful and positive impact within my community by giving my ultimate best."

-JLB

Leadership Qualities

GROWTH MINDSET
Have a growth mindset. Similar to learning new skills, cheers, routines. Always staying open and positive will allow us to learn and grow.

CONTRIBUTE
Be a contributor. Contribute to the team, classmates, co-workers, school, community, world. Contribute your heart, your ideas, and your energy toward making a positive impact.

BE HUMBLE
Yes, it is great when we accomplish a goal, but think of it as benefiting the whole team, empowering the whole community. Face criticism constructively and learn from it.

BE ACTIVE
Be active. Share and delegate duties to others with participation. This shows support for others.

RECOGNITION
Recognize others achievements and skills, abilities and strengths. Note their positive points and give appreciation!

CREATE
Create conditions as an opportunity to motivate others to flourish. Having creativity gives the opportunity of something new to be created within the world.

PROACTIVE
Be proactive. Actively thinking two steps ahead for ways to improve a situation or to prevent a problem from happening allows us to think before we act and make a proper decision.

KNOWLEDGE
Seeking out and learning knowledge from others allows us to make informed and pure decisions, which will help elevate everyone and the desired goal.

POSITIVE MINDSET

PRESENT

HUMBLE

ACTIVE

PROACTIVE

MOTIVATE

KNOWLEDGE

CREATE

How does one be a positive role model in society? By showcasing kind actions within your work, your passions, and your heart to the community. Even if your passion is simply creating positivity in the world. For example, build a flower stand and give out flowers in your community. This demonstrates how to give out positive energy to the community! Create a tribe who demonstrates the heart's intentions and spread the kindness throughout society. This week, I would like for you to give out 5 random acts of kindness. At the end of the week, ask yourself if you feel happier!

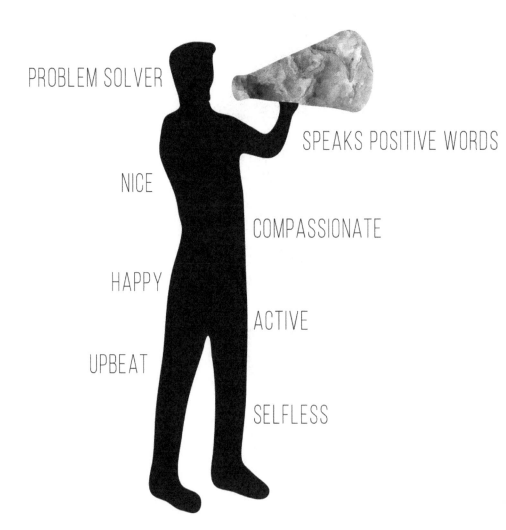

PROBLEM SOLVER

SPEAKS POSITIVE WORDS

NICE

COMPASSIONATE

HAPPY

ACTIVE

UPBEAT

SELFLESS

Common Courtesy Tips

Lead by example.

Saying thank you to someone who has done something nice to you no matter who it is.

Saying excuse me instead of um.

First impressions are key! Making eye contact with a smile.

Compliments: only with sincerity and when you mean it.

Be friendly, cheerful, and polite.

Nice confident handshake.

Be on time.

Punctual.

Let others go first.

Respect one's personal space.

Respecting one's opinion as their opinion and does not define your opinion.

Pink Out

Who remembers the PINK OUT games to bring breast cancer awareness? A Pink Out game is where everyone, including the team, fans, and coaches wears pink in honor of those who lives were effected by breast cancer. The Pink Out games included pink everything, making it so fun and meaningful. This concept is bringing the collaboration of celebrations and giving back into ONE! Service of the heart is the greatest gift of all as it is the passageway of obtaining ultimate joy. The point of celebrating life is to celebrate life in general for everyone.

A billion years ago, humankind did not exist. We have been chosen to experience such a phenomenon of being the humankind. Humankind is a compound word, of human and kind. We as humans must sprinkle kindness around the world with abundance because it is part of us. Pink Out is a brilliant concept of celebrating life in a very kind way of having humans as a whole uplift each other, celebrating life. Pink Out games are so fun, right?!

Fulfilling Universal Needs=FUN

FUN can stand for Fulfilling Universal Needs, which simply means to give back to the parts of our beautiful world that is in need of help. FUN is an acronym for something so much more. Fulfilling Universal Needs is elevating empowerment, spirituality, and peace, which allows us to really engage and connect with our world. We have an energetic connection with one another, making us wired to care for one another. From holidays to brithdays, there are so many different types of celebrations happening year round! Now wouldn't it be awesome if we combined giving back to our world during these special times? Not only yearly celebrations, but also, we can combine the concept with any type of event, show, game, or anything! I would like for you to channel into your spirit and think of different organizations that really reach out to you!

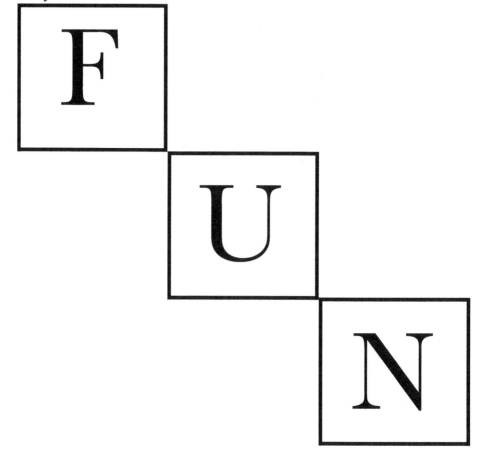

HOW CAN WE MAKE FUN IMPACT?

_____

_____

_____

_____

_____

_____

Interested in being involved with a non-profit, but don't know where to start? Let's look up some non-profits that really pull your attention! Some examples of non-profits include food banks, animal shelters, environmental clean-ups, global relief teams, veterans, homeless, access to care, and so many more! Let's get involved and even try to contribute the F.U.N concept to organizations that really pull our heart strings!

Name of local organization:
    Ways to become involved:
    Ways to spread their message:
    Let's brainstorm a F.U.N strategy:

Name of global organization:
    Ways to become involved:
    Ways to spread their message:
    Let's brainstorm a F.U.N strategy:

"I cheer for others and encourage them to be brave to reach their highest potential." *-JLB*

Adrenaline & Courage

Cheerleaders take huge, yet practical, risks when learning a new skill or stunt. Cheerleaders are seriously fearless! This quality teaches us how to take a leap of faith and knowing we will be okay, with the right focus and application. At first, we might fail; however, bigger the risk, bigger the impact. It is very common for cheerleaders to fail when learning a new skill. I suggest to be very open to this concept of failing and rejection throughout life. Rejection provides direction and opportunity for us to reach what exactly we need to learn. It takes a lot of courage to take a step into an unknown space. On the next page, feel free to journal any courageous acts you may be experiencing within your own life. Write it out and then take a moment to think about what you could be learning from your current situation. From this knowledge, it provides an opportunity to stregthen the courage from within and will take you to all different heights throughout life!

In addition, cheerleaders are drawn to the adrenaline rush of hitting a routine or getting the crowd fired up! It is a strong attraction, and we get hungry for it! The adrenaline rush can be applied to trying something new or different that you have always dreamed about doing. Outside of cheerleading, having courage and adrenaline are huge and important characteristics of experiences throughout life. With the right and safe environment, taking risks and having an adrenaline rush can take you to all different parts of the world.

Journal Entry

Spirit Stick

When I graduated college, I adventured out of the country for my first time ever to Northern India, where the Himalayan Mountains live. I was introduced to several monks and people of the village as I was giving dental treatment to the children of local villages. The village is very remote and has limited access to care. The amount of fulfillment I received from such an experience reminded me of the feeling similar to having a little cheerleader run up to me being so excited about the game in her cheer uniform. The feeling of helping others and inspiring the community truly made my heart fill up with ultimate gratitude. When we cheer at a game, we do not know everyone in the stands, however, the positive energy is flowing all around the community. In the Himalayans, there are prayer flags displayed everywhere, flowing through the air. Prayer flags are colorful rectangular cloths, often found strung along the peaks of the Himalayan Mountains. The flags are used to promote peace, compassion, strength, and wisdom. Prayer flags are not a religion, but are designed to bring good will throughout our world. The wind blows the good will into all aspects of our planet. The different colors of prayer flags symbolize elements of our world.

GREEN- WATER

BLUE- SKY

RED- FIRE

WHITE- AIR

YELLOW-EARTH

When the prayer flags are strung along the peaks, the good will flows into the air and through all parts of our world. Within cheerleading, we have something similar to prayer flags, called a spirit stick. A spirit stick brings a team together and keeps their morale high. Spirit sticks are a symbol of positivity and spirit. It is a reminder of the good will we have within our hearts. The connection between the two is to make the connection of keeping the good will of a cheerleader's heart going throughout our world. Lawrence "Herkie" Herkimer wanted to acknowledge and honor the attitude and enthusiasm of a team, so he created the first spirit stick. A spirit stick must never touch the ground for it is bad luck! A spirit stick can be seen in similarity to prayer flags, which also cannot touch the ground! A spirit stick symbolizes a squads' good will as do prayer flags. I have created a spirit stick with the colors of prayer flags to help one keep the positive spirit and good will with all aspects of our world. Prayer flags are simply a universal sign of compassion and good will. The symbolism between the two releases the power within to channel the positive morale spirit within to all aspects of our planet and life.

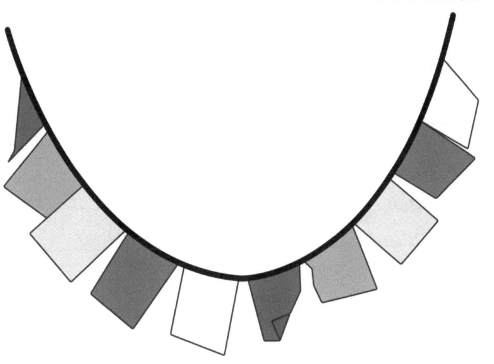

"Never give up
No matter what is going on
Never give up
Develop the heart
Too much energy in your country is spent
developing the mind instead of the heart
Develop the heart,
Be compassionate
Not just to your friends but to everyone,
be compassionate
Work for peace in your heart and in the
world
Work for peace, and I say again
Never give up
No matter what is happening
No matter what is going on around you
Never give up."

-The Dalai Lama

"I am thankful for every single person who comes in my life, for they have a light within that guides the light within myself." *-JLB*

Stunt Groups

Within cheerleading, one of our awesome skills includes stunting. There are multiple different types of stunts, but let's focus on the quad group. A quad group includes two bases, a backspot, and a flyer. Now, everyone has to have balance, stability, strength, and focus, in order for the stunt to hit. Working with a team, it is important for each one of these individuals to have all four qualities, or else it crumbles. In today's society, we are working in more of a "we" community instead of a "me" community. A "we" community brings together the initial quad group, creating a group of like minded individuals bringing in different specialties and gifts to the table. This is the perfect example of a quad group. A quad group can be applied to a friend group, project, outreach, and much more! The goal is to create a quad group, reach out to others, and create an overall team to connect and uplift the community.

Let's take the concept of the quad group. The quad group includes four like minded individuals, who are focused on a goal. The quad groups make up the TRIBE. Your tribe is very important in success. This creates a WE community. A WE community is aWEsome, sWEeet, and poWErful. It is very important to surround yourself with focused and uplifting individuals, because this will allow you to expand the energy out to the community. In a quad group, everyone has to do their part in order for the goal to be achieved. With this concept, I would like for you to find 2-4 other people who can motivate you, keep you focused, like minded, and help you focus on the goal. It can be distracting when people who don't have the same values or mindset as you..It takes energy away from your goals. On the next page, I would like for you to write your core values. Listing your core values helps attract your quad group.

LET'S LIST YOUR CORE VALUES!

_____

_____

_____

_____

_____

_____

_____

_____

_____

_____

_____

_____

Within the group, everyone has the same focus. When deciding the quad group, some will have stronger qualities and talents more or less within the group, which helps decide who will partake in which role. Same concept when creating a group, create a quad group where people can provide strengths where another person of the group cannot. This creates balance and harmony in making overall success! The qualities of a quad group are very important in making a stunt solid. The quad group involves teamwork, meaning everyone must work together. Teamwork makes the dreamwork. Strength is important as it allows us to go from the ground up, hitting our intentions. The quad group is close, meaning they trust each other and are transparent, allowing each other to be close so nothing is shaky or crumbles. Stability creates a stunt to be solid.

Everyone of the stunt group is focused with the right intentions and goals. The stunt group is confident in their actions and in one another to do their part. The stunt group is positive, moving into an upward and positive direction to lift and motivate others. The quad group is present and aware of what is going on within the stunt group and within themselves and their actions. The stunt group is mindful of shifts within the quad group and how to identify and resolve any type of shift to help make the group solid. The flyer is hitting a liberty, which is similar to the Statue of Liberty, who holds on to a torch, which symbolizes to be the light for others. Also, she is holding a book..Which well, is very important as well. The combination of theses qualities creates a very solid "we" community. These characteristics and qualities allows the stunt group to inspire and motivate the community, which is a true treasure of this world

MINDFUL

BE THE LIGHT

BE PRESENT

CONFIDENT

POSITIVE

FOCUS

BALANCE

STABILITY

STRENGTH

CLOSE

TEAMWORK

Everyone within the quad group has to have balance. Balance is key for everyone to make the quad group hit their stunt. To balance or to center yourself, one must practice strength. How do we get strength? Proper rest, healthy foods, healthy mindset. This concept can be applied outside of cheerleading. I have found myself not feeling balanced when I don't have enough rest or eat out more than a couple times a week. Balancing yourself can include meditation, spending time with nature or a pet, reading positive books, and spending time with loved ones. During a stunt, having balance is key for everyone, not just the flyer. Having balance within oneself can be applied outside of the stunt group. Having balance includes taking care of yourself. Balancing work and life. Having a work-life balance is so important for us to do our best in all aspects of life.

Focus

Everyone is focused. Their mind is clear and have the same intentions. Focusing on a goal is key, the focus creates a magnetic connection of thought to action. Focus allows us to use the energy we have inside our mind and apply it directly to the goal desired.

Stability

Everyone within the quad group must have stability to do their part in hitting a solid stunt. Stability within oneself helps create trust. It is important to feel stable or grounded within oneself by finding grounding solutions. Walking with nature, knowing we are all part of the same heart line shows that we are all connected, which creates stability within oneself.

Strength

The strength to persevere to accomplish the goal of hitting the stunt! Mental strength and physical strength, are both used in a stunt. This concept can be applied to life when we are trying to accomplish goals. Have a strong mind and body allows us to help others and accomplish our goals.

Stickability

Within a stunt group, we are always making sure we "stick" our stunts, meaning to persevere and cleanly hit our vision of the stunt. This is important in every day life to be "stickable." Being clear with the goal creates a confidence and attraction of being "stickable," which gains attraction and connection. Being "stickable" creates one to be accountable for their intention is clear to hit the goal! This type of accountability goes a long way! Being accountable means people can rely on you, which creates trust.

"I dream boldly, trusting my mind, body, and soul connects with the universe above, making my dreams come true."

-JLB

Bows to Toes
Dress to Impress

Freshly washed white cheer shoes, teased hair with a pinned bow to perfection is just the tip of the iceberg of the appearance of a cheerleader. We have matching socks, matching bows, wrinkle free uniforms, make-up done, hair done, fluffed poms. YOU NAME IT! Everything is well put together. The professionalism demonstrated here can be applied to professionalism being presented outside of cheer. When attending an interview, career, event, or conference, we must apply this concept in presenting ourselves very professionally. Making sure the wardrobe is looking sharp with a great attitude and smile knocks it out of the park in the majority of social settings! The smile, demeanor, and positive "aura" are important parts of the cheerleading "wardrobe." This cheer mindset leaves a large positive impression with everyone who we come into contact with. A positive aura is a very important part of a successful wardrobe. To create such a vibrant glow, it is important to practice self-care daily! There are different ways to practice self-care to really boost the aura, energy, and attitude! Practicing self-care allows us to give more to others.

CONFIDENT

PRESENT

SMILE

SHARP

POSITIVE AURA

CLEAN

FRESH

SELF CARE TIPS

PHYSICAL

Reduce stress, plenty of sleep, healthy foods and beverages, medical and dental check-ups, daily exercise, stretching. Walking outside.

SPIRIT

Practice gratitude, meditation, nourish the soul, give thanks. Connect with nature. Reduce noise and distractions.

SOCIAL

Connect with like-minded people, connect with positive individuals, volunteer in helping others. Spend time with friends. Check in with family members. Chat with a close friend instead of suppressing emotions.

MINDSET

Positive mindset, continuing personal growth, educating oneself, practice mindfulness, engaging into new experiences. Self-development.

HEART

Be aware of your emotions, what you are feel ing, acknowledging the feelings and being thankful for them, trusting the universe to be on our side. Continue to cultivate a heart of compassion, love, and kindness for yourself and for others.

Write your personal self-care practice!

_____

_____

_____

_____

_____

_____

_____

_____

_____

_____

_____

_____

_____

Yes C stands for Cheerleading! But also.....

Yes, C stands for cheerleading, which of course, is absolutely amazing! But also, there are several words that begin with C that are extremely valuable. The C allows us to SEE clearly and make accurate decisions. Throughout my adventures with life, the qualities below have helped guide me along my path. Let's learn about the C concepts so we can clearly see our path before us.

Character

Character is very important. Trusting our intuition and gut allows us to make choices clearly. Character is what makes us each unique and allows us to release our inner power to the world around us. Making the right decision is never easy, however, our character is what separates us into making positive change and respect for ourself. There are times when something could sound absolutely amazing, but actually isn't what's best for us! For example, let's use a very simple ingredient, sugar. Sugar is super sweet and we use it for almost every holiday! Sugar can be used in all different ways. One way sugar can be used is as a treat. Our society loves to use sugar; however, it isn't all that healthy for us. With this being said, something might sound appealing; however, it is important to take a step back and think about the outcomes. If there is a little voice inside of you, that may be second guessing or questioning the situation, trust it, tap into it, and think about what the voice is saying. Think it out. It might be saving you from something down the road!

Communication

Communication is key in making sure the message is delivered correctly to one another, the community, our world. Communication allows us to connect, collaborate and gain clarity. Communication is very important with anything! Within cheerleading, we have very clear communication from calling out chants to which time-out cheer will be performed during the next time out. Communication is so important in hitting stunts and selecting cheers. We must have clear communication to set the intention. The intention of yelling out a specific cheer teaches the value of communication. We must have the same clear communication throughout all aspects of life.

Courage

Courage is very valuable when we take risks. We have to have courage to make the jump. The jump into the unknown while using what we know as a guide. Similar to learning a tumbling skill. We must have the courage to try the tumbling skill. Courage allows us to make calculated risks to try something new. Courage is stepping out of fear, removing distractions and taking small steps of action towards our goal.

Change

Change is always going to happen within our lifetime. Similar to a new squad every year, some teammates may graduate, some may decide not to cheer anymore, some will transfer from different schools or gyms, whatever the season may be..It allows us to accept how people in general will come in and out of our lives. Some relationships will last a lifetime, and some relationships may last just for a season. Whatever the time frame may be, we must always be extremely thankful to share an exciting moment of time with whoever is currently present within our life. For the longest time, I had a very hard time accepting people flowing out of my life. When a moment is so great and magical, it was hard for me to grasp why it doesn't last. This has taught me to be extremely present and full of gratitude for every moment, situation, and person who is in my life at that moment. With cheerleading, it was always so hard at the end of the season. However, it's the light and qualities of such an experience or a person, who will continue to shine throughout my spirit. It reminds us to not take anything for granted, truly being thankful for the moment. Change will always happen as we are always evolving, growing, and transitioning throughout life. It is important to be open to change, open to the magical space of opportunity that is waiting for us.

Commitment

When we commit to something, the commitment allows us to create stability and trust in creating success. Commitment allows people to count on us making us reliable and trustworthy. Commitment allows a plan to go into action. It it is important to have commitment with our words and actions For example, being committed to ourself, committed to others, committed to what we say, committed to our morals, committed to our spirit. Holding commitment brings us strength and stability. Commitment creates a foundation For example, being committed in a stunt group creates a strong foundation If everyone commits to their actions and duty, the stunt group is solid. The stunt group doesn't crumble or wobble. Commitment allows us to share our personal qualities and instills trust in others and the group.

Confidence

Confidence is a MAJOR SUCCESS SKILL! Within cheerleading, we must have confidence with our skills. We see ourselves hitting the skill, displaying confidence in our actions. During a game, we have our shoulders back strong stance, chin up, smile on our face, loud confident voice, which shows confidence to the crowd. Confidence builds trust and attracts people to you. What's the difference between confidence and arrogance? Confidence leads to positive outcomes, arrogance leads to negative outcomes. On the next page, have listed qualities of a confident individual! I would like for you to choose some of the qualities you feel like you need to work more on! I would like for you to practice these qualities throughout social situations.

Confidence Skills

-POSITIVE THINKER
-CHARISMATIC
-WALKS WITH PURPOSE
-ABUNDANCE MINDSET GIVER
-ACCEPTS OTHERS DIFFERENCES
-SMILES OFTEN
-RELAXED
-DOWN TO EARTH
-GAINS PERSPECTIVE
-OPEN MINDED
-GIVES COMPLIMENTS
-ADMITS MISTAKES
-NEVER TALKS BAD ABOUT OTHERS
-CAN LAUGH AT THEMSELVES
-SELF-LOVE

"The amount of gratitude within my heart is infinite. I will shine my positive light to others with a cheerful smile and kind heart."

-JLB

Coaches & Mentors

The relationships with my coaches have been extremely influential. The amount of gratitude I have towards them is infinite. Coaches teach us to surround ourselves with positive leaders and role models. Leaders who are impacting the world, in some shape or form and really making a difference in the community. Coaches are very influential teachers who help us learn to become better at what we love to do! Coaches connect, strategize, and support us in so many different ways. Coaches believe in the best of us and are true treasures of our world. The amount of gratitude I have towards my coaches goes beyond the stars for they are shining lights who have guided me throughout life. It is always important to understand how coaches and mentors are there to guide us, motivate us, and encourage us. With their guidance, we must be extremely thankful for them. We must always keep in mind how we are responsible for the work we put into anything we do. Coaches and mentors are excellent teachers; however, it is important to understand one must put in their own personal work to achieve one's goal. The combination of personal ambition and excellent coaches and mentors help light the path of a beautiful journey.

Having positive coaches and mentors is very important outside of cheer as well. When looking for a mentor, one may feel nervous of what "value" they have to offer to a mentor. If you feel as if you have nothing to offer for someone you hope to become a mentor, the best advice is to channel your enthusiasm and simply ask, "How can I help?" Enthusiasm with a helping hand go a very long way and I'm sure anyone would appreciate it! Due to working and talking with my coaches, I have learned how to develop a very professional and mature demeanor. Speaking with coaches, athletic directors, marketing crew, production crew in a respectful, genuine, and positive demeanor builds strong connections and relationships.

"Surround yourself only
with people
who are going
to take you
higher."
— Oprah Winfrey

It's Game Day!

L adies and gentlemen, it's game day! That's right. The time where we apply all of our skills, including time management, teamwork, skills, marketing, public relations...You name it! We apply the pep in our step and making it the best day ever. Game day is such an exciting time and truly creates an abundance of fulfillment. From everything to displaying our skills, connecting with the community, and creating ultimate positive energy throughout the day, it is literally everything. This is the time where we have all of our skills shine together. The energy and drive within the day is so motivating and empowering. A lot of the skills and attitude can be applied to outside of game day and into a work day. The energy and drive connects us to our team, community, and coaches making it an overall great day. We can relate game day to a work day in many different ways! Let's go!

Game Day = Work Day
1st Half= 1st Part of Day
Halftime=Lunch
2nd Half= 2nd Part of Day

Time Management

Managing time is huge! We only have so many hours in a day. Working with a proactive, efficient, and clear intention allows us to make the most of our day. Arriving 15 minutes early is being on time. With practices, games, events, our coach always told us to be there 15 minutes early as rule of thumb. It is important to time manage within the work day. Being on time shows respect and value to the client. It is important to perform daily tasks while being respectful of others' time.

Marketing

Cheerleaders are vital to the marketing deck! The excitement and empowering energy we bring to our community is all part of marketing a high energy atmosphere. The same application can be applied to a company or agency. Geniality, smiling, positivity, and a strong work ethic demonstrate how there is a passion to uplift and provide solutions to the community. Out of all, the best marketing skill I can recommend is integrity, honesty, and respect in the most authentic way possible. Being presentable at a game is the same as being presentably at a job. A fresh clean uniform with a genuine smile and positive attitude are all part of representing a team.

Teamwork

Teamwork makes the dreamwork as we all know! Communicating with one another allows us to accomplish goals and present ourselves well. Teamwork creates the foundation of a company, team, or group. This allows us to apply our strengths to one another to become the best we can be as a team! It is very important to keep in mind how we do not compete with one another, as we do root for one another to be the best that they can be. In addition, teamwork teaches us how to work with one another even though there may be some differences present amongst teammates. Teamwork teaches us to set aside any differences and focus on the main intention of the team's goal. This can be applied into the work field as many have different lifestyles and perspectives. This concept allows us to accept one another's unique gifts, set aside any conflicting differences, and channel our attention into the team's goal. Throughout the years of cheerleading, there is always a new team every year with new individuals. This gives us the ability to adapt and work well with others. Whenever one engages into a new project, event, or career, the "new team" philosophy allows us to have an open mind, adjust and add effort where the energy will be most beneficial in accomplishing the overall goal of the team.

Community Interaction

During game time, cheerleaders interact with fans, coaches, and team members while keeping an eye on the clock. Being able to do this teaches us how to connect with the community, employers, and team while being aware of time! In addition, it is important to always maintain a positive attitude. One of the things some squads may do during a game is to start the WAVE with the crowd! The wave creates a fun and positive environment amongst the community. The wave is when a section of the crowd stands up and throws their hands in the air flowing to the next section of the crowd. It creates a "WAVE" effect amongst the crowd, creating a flow of excitement. The wave concept is an example of how positive community interaction can flow through the environment, creating a ripple effect of positivity through one another!

"I cheer for the community to take action in improving our world in the most positive way possible."

-JLB

Self-Discipline

We have several duties during game day as we do with a work day. Within cheerleading, we are self-disciplined by being on time, eating healthier foods, and attending work outs and practices. We are focused and self-disciplined in succeeding in all areas of cheerleading. We can apply this within life by making the overall day a success. Self-discipline teaches us to hold ourself to a certain personal standard. Being able to say no to things teaches us to be self-disciplined. Small actions of self-discipline creates better quality of life.

Flexibility

We understand if a stunt does not hit or go to plan, that we keep going no matter what with a smile on our face. Being flexible at work, allows us to be flexible with others or a situation and to always remain positive and professional. It is important to accept if something does not go exactly to plan, we must be flexible and adapt while maintaining a positive attitude.

Execution

How do we execute a routine? Practice, practice, practice. We work out extra hard in the gym, so we can perform our skills better. We practice our routines, stunts, tumbling, and skills to make the overall routine perfect. With tasks within the workforce, it is important we apply the same concept. Taking extra classes to gain knowledge about a specific skill within our careers, projects, events, allows us to execute skills needed within our projects, careers, and events.

L-E-T-S G-O!

L et's Go! Let's Go! L-E-T-S G-O! Let's Go! Enthusiasm and motivation are two very important factors in cheerleading, as we all know! A key characteristic of cheerleading is enthusiasm. Enthusiasm uplifts people, the environment, the energy. Enthusiasm is fundamental in connecting high positive energy with high positive energy found within others and our world. Scientifically, our bodies are made of cells, which include atoms made of high vibrating energy. From the way we think, talk, work, dream, and believe are all forms of expression of our personal energy. Energy is everywhere around us and a part of us, and using positive energy is very important in maintaining a connection with ourselves, the world, and the universe to give us those positive outcomes we desire. The energy channeled by a powerhouse go-getter mindset with an emphasis on positivity and dedication can be magical by making huge impact on the world. So let's get fired up with enthusiasm and LET'S GO! We are always motivating and cheering for others, which is fantastic. But not only do we cheer for others, we cheer for ourselves too. I would like for you to become your own inner personal cheerleader for your goals and your life. Having a "Let's Go" mindset encourages everyone around you and those who you wish to lead! The components of the Let's Go Equation includes: goal setting, enthusiasm, dedication, and developing a work ethic. Positive cheers and chants emphasize the enthusiasm mindset. Dedication and a strong work ethic give you the tools to execute those goals. Once you have the "Let's Go!" mentality, you can accomplish anything!

THE LET'S GO EQUATION

Setting a Goal + Enthusiasm + Dedication + Work Ethic

Halftime Performance

During a halftime performance, our overall goal is to hit the routine perfectly. Within the routine, there are stunts, dances, tumbling, and jumps. With this being said, there are microsteps that are needed to accomplish each skill to make the overall performance AMAZING! We can think of the halftime performance as your overall vision for the year. Let's apply this concept outside of cheer. Let's treat each goal as skills within a halftime performance. When we begin to learn a Halftime routine, it is innovative and slowly comes together. Let's try this with creating new goals. Innovative means creating something new. Think about five goals you would like to set for the year and how each goal will need microsteps to accomplish the overall performance. Microsteps are the foundation of creating anything! Small victories lead to large victories. Step by step, motion by motion, we can create the most amazing purposeful routine.

Once we have set our goals and microsteps, we have to visualize ourselves doing it, similar as if we were to hit a stunt or land a jump. Visualizing ourselves achieving a goal shows that the goal is tangible, meaning it is perceptible by touch. Applying the laws of attraction will connect with the energy around us and turn your goals into reality!

Now within a halftime performance, there are several transitions being accomplished throughout the overall performance. During a halftime performance, we go through multiple transitions. From within a stunt sequence or from the dance section to tumbling skills, we are constantly making transitions. These transitions have focus. We can apply this concept to transitions within life. There are always life changes and transitions that we go through. It is part of life. With life transitions, it is important to maintain focus on our goals, same as within a halftime performance. This concept can be applied to reaching an overall vision for the year, we must maintain focus through life's transitions.

Halftime Performance Equals Overall Vision

Each goal needs microsteps to accomplish the goal, similar to hitting the different skills of the halftime performance. To reach each goal, it takes resilience, hard work, strength, practice, and patience. Focusing on each microstep allows us to take the steps necessary to reach the goal. Accomplishing these different goals allows us to reach the overall project, vision, goal, or business.

Goal 1 symbolizes stunts.
Goal 2 symbolizes dance.
Goal 3 symbolizes tumbling.
Goal 4 symbolizes cheers.
Goal 5 symbolizes jumps.

Once you have your goals written down, I would like for you to take out another piece of paper. Next, you will write out your goals and tape it to a door or mirror you see everyday. Attraction gains attraction. Focus on it every day, think about it, and FEEL it within yourself as if you have already accomplished the goal!

With accomplishing a goal, a lot of failure is involved. This is all part of the process. When we first learn how to do a cheerleading skill, we usually fail A LOT! We practice and practice, learning what to do differently and taking action into microsteps to reach a goal. For example, if we are learning a cheer and we are not remembering the cheer and motions easily, we break up the cheer into sections, going over those microsteps over and over again until we have muscle and verbal memory of that first section. Then from there, we will add on a few more motions that are part of the overall cheer. We will continue to go step by step until we have the whole cheer memorized reaching the overall goal of learning the cheer.

For a goal, we will have to break it down into micro-movements into accomplishing the overall goal. Within cheerleading, we focus our intention on hitting whichever skill we are focusing on. The concept can be applied to setting a goal we wish to achieve at the moment. We zone our focus into achieving our goal. Saying words such as, "I am healthy" or "I am productive" states as if we have already achieved the goal, which teaches our minds to focus in on achieving the goal. Being clear and direct with our statements allows us to connect with the universe and our goals. With every jump, tumbling skill, stunt, dance, and cheer, we apply action and energy. Close your eyes and envision yourself accomplishing your skill or goal, see yourself accomplishing it!

Next, apply action and energy into the microsteps to accomplish your goals. You have everything inside of you to accomplish your goals. The positive and dynamic mindset, high energy drive, passionate heart, and strong focus creates the magic of accomplishing your goals! Similar to a cheer team, it is important to surround yourself with teammates, a quad group, or uplifting individuals. It allows us to dedicate ourselves and feel motivated into accomplishing our goals.

GOAL #1
    -microstep:
    -microstep:
    -microstep:
GOAL #2
    -microstep:
    -microstep:
    -microstep:
GOAL #3
    microstep:
    -microstep:
    -microstep:
GOAL #4
    -microstep:
    -microstep:
    -microstep:
GOAL #5
    -microstep:
    -microstep:
    -microstep:

Let's Make Positive Impact!

I would like for you to channel your goals into positive impact. A tip in designing a truly successful goal, is to have three solid positive benefits for the world. If you can provide three points of why something benefits someone in a very confident, yet genuine manner, SUCCESS will follow. From your goals, select one and explain how it can create three positive benefits for the world. Your goal may be to design a product, service, or event. Your goal may even be as simple as reading a book a month. How can this goal help others. Reading a book, for example, a benefit could be to share your knowledge learned from the book to others. Your goal might be to design clothes. How could we benefit others through this idea. For example, designing clothes to help one to feel confident. Another benefit could be for each item sold, the company will give 30% back to a charity. For whatever, the goal may be, I would like for you to write three ways it can create positive impact.

Goal:
Benefit 1:
Benefit 2:
Benefit 3:

Hands on Hips, Smiles on Lips!

Now with every goal, I would like for you to know this goal is part of your super hero powers. The combination of super powers and positivity helps one reach their goal. I would like for you to place your hands on your hips as if we were standing on the sidelines before a halftime performance. This is your super hero stance. Your bow symbolizes being present, the smile creates positivity flowing, and the arms symbolize confidence. The super hero pose creates empowerment within one's self to release inner magic. From the super hero pose, I would like for you to raise your hands up to high V for 2 minutes and say I GOT THIS 3x as if it was cheer!

PRESENT

SMILE

CONFIDENCE

SUPER HERO POSE

The "Clean" Concept

When we perform a cheer, stunt, or routine, we use very clean and sharp motions. The "clean" factor creates organization and execution, allowing us to present our message clearly to the crowd. A "clean" performance is very organized and focused. Have a clean routine, allows us to present what we would like to present very clearly, having the message easy to understand.

The clean concept can be applied in all aspects of life. Either in our home environment, with a resume, work environment, self-care, food choices, mindset, and energy..The cleaner, the lighter, the better! Let's adventure into how we can make some of these categories more "clean."

With a "clean" mindset, we know it takes timing, self-discipline, and focus. As we know with a routine, the cleaner the routine, the more success we display! The end result of a solid halftime show is the way it is executed and presented. In addition, the clean concept can be applied to presenting your overall vision, the halftime performance. Clean, sharp, dynamic, and executed is exactly how a solid routine is accomplished! On the next page are ways to apply the "clean" concept in different ways!

Home Environment
-Let go of anything that is not being used.
-Simplify and donate what is not needed.
-Let go of anything that does not make you happy.
-Maintains overall tidy and clean home environment.

Career
-Clean and organized work environment.
-Complete tasks more efficiently.
-Clear communication with clients and team.
-Clean uniform and overall hygienic.

Food Choices
-Eat clean organic foods.
-Less intake of processed foods and sugars.
-Drink more water.
-Cook at home.

Environment
-Recycle as much as possible and reduce use of plastic.
-Use reusable containers, straws, bags, etc.
-Choose more eco-friendly food options.
-Creates clean environment by setting up group clean-ups.

Megaphones

The microsteps elevate us to reach a goal, which creates the entire megaphone. Each little step takes us closer and closer to impact others. The reason why a megaphone was created was to reach out to more people, to cheer louder, to elevate the energy. There are so many ways to use a megaphone within our life. We can use a megaphone to share our goals and insights with the world by reaching out to more people. The megaphone is used in cheerleading to chant out to the crowd, motivating the entire crowd to have positive spirit. Not only is the megaphone used to motivate the crowd, but also it is elevating the energy and inspiring others with our message and goals. With your goals, I would like for you to write out the microsteps needed to take action to accomplish your overall goal. Once you reach your goal, share with others, inspire others, spread your message to uplift society! Motivate others to pursue their dreams and continue to motivate your community into living a cheerful life.

ELEVATE

Positive energy is positive, a plus sign. A plus sign rises and elevates. The energy connects with the world around us. I would like for you to raise your arms up to the sky with excitement and let the happy spirit within your heart release up to the universe!

Combining positive energy with work ethic elevates our thoughts and dreams with the stars above and into reality. Now, what are you going to do with this magical power? We rise by lifting others, elevating one another to our highest self. I am cheering for you to use your magical gift in uplifting society. Cheerleaders are a bright and vital light in this world. I truly believe you are going to really help the world in a variety of ways.

Always, it is important to put a greater emphasis on being a good human more than anything. The positive mindset, strong work ethic, high adrenaline, genuine heart, within yourself is going to connect you in so many different positive ways with the world and will continue to make a positive impact for our planet! Always remember, the bow represents to be present, be present with every minute of your life. You are a true gift of this magical world!

Being present and sharing your unique gift with the world will help create an absolutely amazing impact. Elevating one another with our special gifts connects and uplifts one another, which is true magic. When we connect, uplift, and elevate our world on a positive level, we are not only enriching our lives, but also creating a wonderful world for the future generations and our beloved planet. The light within connects with the lights above in the sky, creating a glow within that magically connects us with one another.

From my heart to yours,
elevate your spirit.

Empowering Affirmations

I AM FIERCE, FOCUSED, AND FLEXIBLE!

I AM FULL OF POSITIVE & AUTHENTIC LEADERSHIP!

I AM FULL OF SPIRIT & POSITIVE ENERGY!

I AM INCREDIBLY FEARLESS!

I AM
GOOD
ENOUGH!

I AM ALWAYS RESPECTFUL OF OTHERS!

I AM
A POSITIVE
LIGHT WITHIN
THIS WORLD!

I AM GIVING TO OTHERS WHO NEED HELP!

I AM BRAVE AND COURAGEOUS IN ALL ASPECTS OF MY LIFE!

I AM WORTHY AND RESPECTFUL OF MYSELF!

I AM CHEERFUL FOR EVERY MOMENT OF MY LIFE!

I AM FULL OF CREATIVITY AND IMAGINATION!

I AM DYNAMIC AND INTERESTING!

I AM FULL OF KINDNESS, BEAUTY, AND INTELLIGENCE!

I AM DRIVEN BY MY PASSIONATE HEART AND STRONG WORK ETHIC!

I AM ALWAYS LOOKING OUT FOR OTHERS IN NEED OF A HELPING HAND!

Meet Rachel of Rachel Elizabeth Design!

As former cheermates and co-captains, Rachel and Jordan always worked well with each other! It is an honor to have Rachel part of this book, for we truly want to inspire others and to always live a cheerful life! Currently, Rachel is the owner of Rachel Elizabeth Design. Rachel is an artist and designer based in Chicago, Illinois. Rachel grew up in a very small town in the Midwest. She fell in love with cheerleading at 5 years old and continued cheerleading through college at Southern Illinois University in Carbondale, IL. Rachel believes cheerleading is the perfect outlet to gain confidence, to learn how to be a team member, and to motivate others. Her artwork is a product of her adventurous and feminine style, which is inspired by travel, music, social interaction, and surprising color combinations. Rachel travels internationally and uplifts the world by her amazingly positive personality and incredibly beautiful artwork! Please discover more at www.rachelelizabeth.design.